Legends
of the
Masters

Legends of the Masters

From the Age of Heroes for
the Martial Artist of Today

Kris Wilder and
Lawrence A. Kane

©2015 Kris Wilder & Lawrence A. Kane

Stickman Publications, Inc.
Burien, WA 98146

Cover art, design and interior layout by Kami Miller
Interior art elements by Kris Wilder

All rights reserved. Reproduction of any part or the whole of this work in any form without prior written permission from the copyright owners is prohibited. No part of this publication may be reproduced, stored in or introduced into a retrieval system, or transmitted in any form or by any means (electronic, mechanical, photocopying, recording, or otherwise), without authorization. To request the authors' consent to reproduce any portions of this work please contact the authors through their website at:
www.westseattlekarate.com.

ISBN-13: 978-0692371626
ISBN-10: 0692371621

Disclaimer

This is a work of fiction. All names, characters, situations, locations, and incidents are either the product of the author's fevered imaginations or are used fictitiously. Any resemblance to genuine persons, living, dead, or undead, or to actual places, events, businesses, or organizations, is entirely coincidental. Information in this book is distributed "As Is," without warranty. Nothing in this document constitutes a legal opinion nor should any of its contents be treated as such. Neither the authors nor the publisher shall have any liability with respect to information contained herein. Further, neither the authors nor the publisher have any control over or assume any responsibility for websites or external resources referenced in this book.

Table of Contents

1. The Malicious Old Master	1
2. The Masters and the Bear	3
3. Two Masters and a Tyrant	5
4. A Master without his Braid	7
5. The Master and his Quarrelling Disciples	9
6. The Disciple and the Fox	11
7. The Disciple and the Grapes	13
8. The Old Master and the Dishonest Doctor	15
9. The Mischievous Disciple	17
10. The Master and the Pilfering Groom	19
11. The Bloodthirsty Brigand and the Disciple	21
12. The Master and the Innkeeper's Son	23
13. The Cutpurse, the Thief, and the Master	25
14. The Burglar and the Master	27
15. Two Masters at the Arena	29
16. The Avaricious Woodsman and the Master	31
17. The Master and the Water Pitcher	33
18. The Boastful Master	35
19. The Young Disciple and the Nettles	37
20. The North Wind, the Sun, and the Master	39
21. The Master and his Otiose Disciples	41
22. The Vainglorious Disciple and the Milk Pail	43
23. The Master, the Merchant, and the Thief	45
24. The Blind Master and the Cub	47
25. The Master and the Thirsty Hooligan	49
26. The Disciple and the Cook	51
27. The Drowning Disciple and his Negligent Master	53
28. Two Masters and a Thief	55
29. The Master and the Inept Doctor	57
30. The Two Bags	59
31. The Disciple and the Filberts	61
32. Two Masters at the Spring	63
33. A Disciple on the Housetop	65
34. The Master and the Viper	67
35. The Master and the Whetstone	69
36. A Disciple and the Fearsome Master	71
37. The Townsmen and the Brigands	73
38. The Wagoner and the Master	75

39. The Image Seller and the Master	77
40. The Cavalryman, his Horse, and the Master	79
41. Three Brigands and a Guileful Master	81
42. The Horse and His Rider	83
43. The Elderly Master and his Churlish Liege Lord	85
44. The Compassionate Master and the Wolf	87
45. The False Prophet and the Master	89
46. The Captured Drummer	91
47. The Disciple, the Thief, and the Magistrate	93
48. The One-Eyed Master	95
49. The Starving Master and the Jewel	97
50. The Fool and the Master	99
51. The Cobbler turned Doctor and the Master	101
52. The Master, the Disciple, and the Plane Tree	103
53. The Master and the Hare	105
54. The Disciple and his two Sweethearts	107
55. The Master and the Bandit Lord	109
56. The Master and the Fearsome Warrior	111
57. The Stargazing Disciple	113
58. By the Company he Keeps	115
59. The Bald Master	117
60. The Master and his Dog	119
61. A Warrior in Love	121
62. Brigands, the Townsfolk, and the Master	123
63. The Disciple and the Swan	125
64. The Master, the Disciple, and the Ant	127
65. The Imposter	129
66. The Bandit Chief and his Disciples	131
67. The Old Master and The Grim Reaper	133
68. The Disciple and his Shadow	135
69. The Miser and the Master	137
70. Disciples at the River	139
71. The Master who lost his Spade	141
72. The Huntsman, the Master, and the Tracks of the Lion	143
73. The Serpent, the Eagle, and the Master	145
74. The Disciple Chasing a Brigand	147
75. The Widow and the Mendacious Disciple	149
76. The Master and the Horseman	151
77. The Master who was an Oracle	153
78. The Wily Master	155
79. A Master, his Disciple, and the Robbers	157
80. The Master's Indomitable Spirit	159

INTRODUCTION

In the karate dojo, we teach people how to make unnatural body mechanics become normal, helping them relearn fundamentals like moving and breathing—even their flinch reactions—in order to increase their combat effectiveness. Take stances for example, they can be very challenging until karateka get the hang of them. Oftentimes a new student will take too high a stance and we will tell them to get lower, yet the practitioner next to them might respond by getting even lower when they already had the correct height.

By telling folks to, "Be like Goldilocks, not too high and not too low," they instantly understand the proper position, often repeating this "Goldilocks Rule" to others.

This is the essences of communication through story. This is the beauty of myth, of legends, fables, parables, family stories, and even of history. An engaging story told and retold shares a moment, a message, it becomes a meaningful means of communication that can be passed down through the generations.

The master of this form of communication was man named Aesop. Legend tells that he was a slave who became an adviser to kings, an extraordinary man who had gained his freedom through quick wit and a clever mind. It is also said that while his face was ugly, the beauty of his works is timeless.

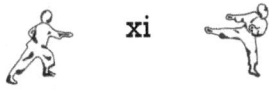

Most of Aesop's true history was lost to time. Some say he was born in Turkey while others believe that he was of African descent. We really don't know much about him as a person, but in many ways we all know him through the assembled writings he left behind, Aesop's Fables.

The fables that he told were not true, of course. Rabbits did not talk to foxes, nor lions to mice, or jackdaws to pigeons for that matter, at least not in English (or Greek, the language that his fables were recorded in). The truth of Aesop's writings were not in the characters found in his stories, but rather in the timeless messages conveyed through his stories.

Some, such as The Boy Who Cried Wolf or The Tortoise and the Hare, are so well known they have become legend. Others, not so much… What we have done herein is retool Aesop's lesser-known fables to better meet the needs and interests of martial artists. The key messages are sacrosanct, why mess with perfection, yet we have reimagined these timeless tales to better suit students of the arts today. It is our sincere hope that you find this re-imaginings useful for your personal studies and, for those of you who teach, for your students' explorations as well.

Enjoy!

1. The Malicious Old Master

A malicious old master, enfeebled by age and no longer able to fight an honorable duel, determined to maintain his fearsome reputation with cunning. Betaking himself to a cave in a wood not far from his town, he lay down inside and feigned to be sick. Whenever any of the other masters entered to inquire after his health, he sprang upon them and beat them senseless. Many stout warriors lost their lives in this way, until one day an astute young master called upon the old master in the cave. Having some suspicion of the truth, the young master addressed his elder from just beyond the entrance, asking how he did. The old master replied that he was indeed in a very bad way, "But," said he, "Why do you stand outside in the cold? Pray come in where it is warm and converse with me." "I should have done so," answered the astute young master, "if I had not noticed that all the footprints point towards the cave yet none exit the other way."

2. The Masters and the Bear

Two masters were traveling on a country road together when a bear suddenly emerged from the woods. The first master immediately made for a tree at the side of the road, climbed up high into the branches, and hid himself there. The second master was not as nimble as his companion. Knowing he could not escape the approaching creature, he threw himself onto the ground and pretended to be deceased. The bear came up and sniffed all around him, yet the master kept perfectly still, all the while holding his breath, for he knew that no bear would molest a dead body. Sure enough, the bear took him for a corpse, chuffed, and wandered away. When the coast was clear, the first master climbed down from the tree and asked the other what it was the bear had whispered to him when it put its mouth to his ear. The second master replied, "He told me never again to travel with someone who deserts a companion at the first sign of danger." With that the second master took his leave from his companion for he had learned the lesson that misfortune often tests the sincerity of friendship.

3. Two Masters and a Tyrant

Two masters were travelling together. One had taken a vow never to speak the truth, whereas the other had sworn to never tell a lie. In the course of their travels they came upon the realm of a narcissistic tyrant who fancied himself king. The tyrant, upon hearing of their arrival, ordered the masters to be brought before him. By way of impressing his guests with his magnificence, the tyrant received them whilst seated upon a gold-wrought throne with the severed heads of his enemies impaled on spikes to either side. His subjects, dressed in all their finery, ranged in long rows before the throne and its grisly bounty.

When the masters came into his presence, the tyrant asked them what they thought of him as a king. The lying master said, "Sire, everyone who knows your eminence must see that you are a most noble and mighty monarch." "And what do you think of my subjects?" continued the despot. "They," spoke the master, "are in every way worthy of their royal sovereign." The tyrant was so delighted with this answer that he gave the master a very handsome reward.

The other master thought that if his companion was rewarded so splendidly for telling a lie, he himself would certainly receive a far greater remuneration for telling the truth. When the tyrant turned to him and asked, "And what, good sir, is your opinion?" the truthful master replied, "I believe that you are a pompous tyrant, and all your subjects are insignificant cowards most deserving of your rule." To his chagrin the unfortunate man discovered that speaking truth to power seldom carries the expected reward, for the tyrant was so enraged by this reply that he ordered the honest master to be taken away and tortured to death.

4. A Master without his Braid

A young master's sole conceit was his long, luxurious hair which he took to combing and braiding daily before the mirror. After a time he discovered that if he wove small blades into his braid he could use it as a fearsome weapon with which to set upon his foes, acquiring no small repute over the years for doing so. Ambushed by brigands one day, he fought his way free only to find that his braid had been cleaved in twain upon an adversary's blade. He was then so much ashamed of his appearance that he thought life could not be worth living unless he could persuade the other masters to part with their braids as well, and thus divert attention from his own loss. By and by he called a meeting of all his fellow masters and advised them to cut off their braids. "They are ugly things anyhow," he proclaimed, "and besides they are heavy when soaked by sky, stream, or sea. Can we all not agree that it is tiresome to be carrying them about?" But his plan was thwarted when one of the other masters replied, "My friend, if you had not lost your own braid you would not be so keen on getting us to cut off ours as well."

5. The Master and his Quarrelling Disciples

A certain master had several disciples who were always quarrelling with one another. Try as he might he could not get them to live together in harmony, so he determined a plan with which to convince them of their folly. Bidding them go into the woods and fetch back a bundle of sticks, he stacked the branches and tied them tightly together. The master then invited each disciple in turn to break the bundle in twain by striking it with their foot or fist. All tried and all failed despite their utmost determination and vigor. When the master then undid the bundle and handed each disciple the sticks one-by-one they had no difficulty in breaking them whatsoever. "There, my disciples," said he, "united you will be more than a match for your enemies, yet if you quarrel and separate your weakness will put you at the mercy of those who wish you harm." Thus chastened, the quarrelling disciples pledge to argue no more.

6. The Disciple and the Fox

A disciple was greatly vexed by a sly fox which came prowling night after night about his master's yard and carried off their prized fowl. So, he set a trap for the scavenging beast and caught him up in it. While it would have been easy to slay the thief in his net at once, the disciple had other things in mind. In order to be revenged upon the fox he tied a bunch of tow to its tail, set fire to it, and let the hapless animal go. As ill-luck would have it, however, the terrified fox made straight under the nearby residence. Ignited by flames from the fox's tail, the building quickly caught fire while those inside, smelling smoke and seeing flame, fled for their very lives. The disciple hung his head in shame as his master's home was burnt into ash before his very eyes, belatedly remembering his master's admonishment that those set to embark upon revenge had best dig two graves.

7. The Disciple and the Grapes

A certain master's disciple, having trained hard all day, was famished. Traveling home he spied some fine bunches of grapes hanging from a vine that was trained along a high trellis and hoped to slake his hunger by eating them. For an hour he did his best to reach them by jumping as high as he could into the air. Over and over again he leapt, but it was all in vain, for they were just out of reach. At last, exhausted, he gave up trying. Walking away with an air of dignity and unconcern he remarked, "I thought those grapes were ripe but I see now they are quite sour and unfit for eating." Pusillanimous men such as this disciple often disdain that which they cannot possess.

8. The Old Master and the Dishonest Doctor

A master in his dotage became almost totally blind from a disease of the eyes. After consulting a doctor, he made an agreement in the presence of witnesses that he should pay the doctor a handsome fee if he was cured of his condition while if the doctor failed he would receive nothing for his efforts. The doctor accordingly prescribed and carried out a course of treatment. Every time he paid a visit, however, the doctor took away with him some article from the master's house until at last when he stopped by for the last time and the cure was complete, there was nothing left inside. When the old master discovered that his house had been robbed of all his worldly possessions he naturally refused to pay the doctor his fee. After repeated refusals on the master's part, the doctor brought a claim before the magistrates for payment of the debt which he claimed he was justly owed.

On being brought into court, however, the wily old master was ready with his defense. "The claimant," said he, "has accurately stated the facts of our agreement. I undertook to pay him a fee if he cured me and he, on his part, promised to charge nothing if he failed. Now, he says unto you that I am cured, but I assert that I am blinder than ever and can prove the truth of my words. When my eyes were failing I could at any rate see well enough to be aware that my house contained a certain amount of furniture and other things of value, but now when according to the doctor I am cured I am entirely unable to see anything inside my home at all."

9. The Mischievous Disciple

There was once a mischievous disciple who used to taunt people and strike out at those around him without any provocation, and thus became a great nuisance to everyone who called upon his master's home. Fed up with these antics, his master fashioned a bell, secured it with a silken cord, and bade the mischievous disciple wear it around his neck to warn people of his presence. Unaware of the true reasons the gift had been bestowed upon him, the disciple was very proud of the bell and strutted about tinkling it with immense satisfaction much to the annoyance of his peers. Finally one day an older student came up to him and said, "The fewer airs you give yourself the better, young man. You are not so foolish to believe, are you, that the bell was awarded in recognition of merit? On the contrary, it is a badge of disgrace." To his great shame the mischievous disciple discovered that notoriety is often mistaken for fame.

10. The Master and the Pilfering Groom

There was once a groom who spent long hours clipping and combing the horse of which he had been given charge, but who daily stole a portion of its allowance of feed and sold it for his own gain. Malnourished, the horse gradually took to worse and worse condition. A traveling master came across the stable looking for a new mount to purchase. After examining the steed that was presented before him he told the groom, "If you truly desire that beast to look sleek and well groomed you must comb him less and feed him more."

11. The Bloodthirsty Brigand and the Disciple

A murderous brigand came upon a very young disciple toiling in his master's field and had some small twinge of conscious given the age of his intended victim. So, he cast about for a grievance with which to justify his bloodlust. "Last week at the tavern you insulted me most abhorrently," spoke the brigand. "That is impossible sir," replied the youth, "For I am far too young to leave my master's residence. I work in the fields in hopes of someday demonstrating my merit such that he will countenance that I may learn the mysteries of his system." "Well," retorted the brigand, "you have stolen food from my hearth." "That cannot be," replied the disciple, "for I have tasted naught but from my master's table according to my needs." "You drink from my spring then," continued the brigand. "Indeed, sir," said the youth, "I have never yet drunk anything but from my master's well." "All this matters not," retorted the brigand, "I shall not depart without unleashing my vengeance." Without further ado he sprang upon the hapless child, running him through with his sword.

12. The Master and the Innkeeper's Son

A certain master, exhausted from his travels, was sound asleep in his room when he was awaked by the innkeeper's son tiptoeing through the chamber. Losing his temper, the master seized the youth by the throat and prepared to strike him down with his fist. The terrified boy piteously entreated the master to spare his life. "I did not mean to awaken you noble sir," he cried. "Please let me go and one day I will repay you for your kindness." The idea of so insignificant a creature ever being able to do anything for him amused the master so much that he laughed aloud, released the boy, and went back to sleep.

Soon enough the boy's chance arrived. One day the master became entangled in a net, captured by vicious brigands who planned to dispose of him with great ceremony and torment come the dawn. The boy who was out in the woods collecting firewood for the inn recognized the master's cries of anger and distress and quickly ran to the spot where the man was held. The boy waited in the nearby bushes until the brigands fell into a drunken stupor, then under cover of darkness set at the ropes with his belt knife. Before long, the master was free. "There!" whispered the boy, "you laughed at me when I promised that I would repay you, but now you see that I have kept my word. Even an innkeeper's son can help a great martial arts master."

13. The Cutpurse, the Thief, and the Master

A cutpurse and a thief went into partnership and sallied out to make their fortune together. Before long a master became aware of their nefarious activities and took it upon himself to put an end to their exploits. The knowledge that the master would soon catch up with them left them both dreadfully frightened and pondering whatever they should do. The thief, thinking that he had divined a method of saving his skin took matters into his own hands. Leaving the cutpurse behind, he sought out the master and boldly said unto him, "I shall manage that you get hold of the cutpurse without the trouble of stalking him if you will promise to let me go free in exchange for my assistance."

The master reluctantly agreed to this and the thief then rejoined his companion, contriving before long to lead him by a hidden pit in the forest which some hunter had dug as a trap for wild animals. A well-timed shove and down into the depths the cutpurse fell. When the master who had been following stealthily behind the pair saw that the cutpurse was safely caught and could not soon escape the pit, it was to the thief that he turned his attention. Drawing his sword he swiftly ran the criminal through with his blade. As

the final breath departed his lips the thief murmured, "I sought to betray a friend, yet it seems that I have only ruined myself." Unabashed, the master then proceeded to finish off the cutpurse.

14. The Burglar and the Master

A certain burglar heard that students in a rich and well-heeled monastery were ailing. So, he went to the marketplace, got himself up as a doctor and, taking with him a newly purchased set of instruments proper to his apparent profession, presented himself at the door. There, he inquired after the health of those inside. "We shall do very well," the master replied without letting him in, "when we have seen the last of you." The burglar, discovering to his chagrin that no matter a villain may disguise himself he will not deceive the wise, trod home poorer than whence he had left.

15. Two Masters at the Arena

Two champions, masters of different styles, were companions on a journey. One was a grappler who specialized in strangulations while the other relied on his fists to reign blows down upon his adversaries. In the course of conversation they began to boast about their prowess and those worthies whom they had defeated in battle, each claiming the superiority of their discipline over that of the other man. They were still arguing with much heat and vigor when they came upon an arena and beheld a statue out front of the stadium that depicted one warrior strangling another.

"There!" proclaimed the first master triumphantly, "look at that. His wrestling technique is much the same as mine! Does this not that prove to you that my style is greater than yours?" "Not so fast, my friend," replied the second master. "That is only your view. If statues could be made to move about on their own you would see one man pummeling the other with lightening blows. Since they are fixed in place the artist simply chose the method that could be depicted most pleasingly. Truly, there are two sides to every question, and this image sheds no more light upon yours than it does mine."

Legends of the Masters

16. The Avaricious Woodsman and the Master

A woodsman who could not swim was felling a tree alongside the bank of a mighty river when his axe, glancing off the trunk, flew out of his hands and fell into the water. As he stood by the river's edge lamenting his loss, a wandering master happened along and asked him the reason for his grief. On learning what had happened, out of pity for the woodsman's distress, the master dived into the river and, bringing up a golden axe, asked him if that was the one he had lost. The woodsman replied that it was not, so the master then dived in a second time. Bringing up a silver axe, he asked if it belonged to the woodsman. "No, that is indeed a handsome axe, but it is soft and malleable hence could not fell a tree. I am afraid that is not mine either," the man replied. Once more the master dove into the river and this time brought up the woodsman's missing axe. The man was overjoyed at recovering his property and thanked his benefactor warmly. The latter was so pleased with the woodsman's honesty that he made him a present of the other two axes before continuing on his travels.

When the woodsman related this story to his companions, one of them was filled with envy at his good fortune and determined to try his luck for himself. So, he went and began to fell a tree at the edge of the river and presently contrived to let his axe drop into the water hoping that the master would arrive. Indeed, the master appeared as before, and on learning that the second woodsman's axe had fallen into the water he dived in and brought up a golden axe even as he had done on the previous occasion. Without waiting to be asked whether or not it was his own the greedy fellow cried, "That's mine, that's mine," and eagerly stretched out his hand for the prize. But, the master was so disgusted at the woodsman's dishonesty that he not only declined to give him the golden axe but also refused to recover for him the one he had let fall into the stream. Turning to leave, the master shoved the avaricious woodsman into the water before continuing on his journey. Soaking wet, humiliated, and lacking the vital tool with which to conduct his trade, the woodsman discovered that honesty is indeed the best policy.

Legends of the Masters

17. The Master and the Water Pitcher

The master toiled day and night to perfect his body, straining so hard that he was no longer able to lift his arms for so greatly had he labored. He had left a pitcher with some water in it nearby to slake his thirst, but had already drunk from it the previous day and discovered that there was so little left that, try as he might, he could not reach the liquid inside with his mouth or tongue. Unable to lift his arms despite a brief respite, it seemed as though he would perish from thirst within sight of the remedy. At last the parched master hit upon a clever plan. He began scooping up nearby pebbles with his mouth and spitting them into the pitcher. With each pebble the water rose a little higher until at last it reached the brim and, thankfully, the knowing master was enabled to quench his thirst. Necessity, he had discovered, was the mother of invention.

18. The Boastful Master

Two illustrious masters of noble birth were on the road together and fell into a dispute as to which of the two was the better born. They kept at it for some time, positing the exploits of their lineage, until at last they came to a place where the road passed through a cemetery full of monuments. There, the first master stopped, looked about him, and heaved a mighty sigh. "Why do you sigh?" queried the second master. The first master pointed to the tombs and replied, "All the monuments that you see here were erected in honor of my forefathers who in their day were eminent men." The second master was speechless for a moment, but quickly recovering replied, "Oh! Do not stop at any lie, good sir. You are quite safe, for I am certain that none of your ancestors will rise up and expose you." Knowing that boasters brag most when they cannot be detected, he separated from his companion and walked away in disgust.

19. The Young Disciple and the Nettles

A young disciple was gathering berries from a bush when his hand was stung by a nettle. Burning with the pain he ran to tell his master. Fighting back tears the boy related, "I only touched it ever so lightly." "That is just why you got stung," the master replied. "If you had grasped it firmly the nettle would not have hurt you in the least." Thus the young disciple learned the lesson to chase after his aspirations with vigor.

20. The North Wind, the Sun, and the Master

A dispute arose between the North Wind and the Sun, each claiming that he was stronger than the other. At last they agreed to competition whereupon they would try their powers upon a traveling master to see which of them could soonest strip him of his cloak. The North Wind had the first try. Gathering up all his force for the attack, he came whirling furiously down upon the man, catching up his cloak as though he would wrest it from him in but one single effort. But, the harder the wind blew the harder the master fought back, closely wrapping his cloak about himself and securing it there with all is considerable strength. Then came the Sun's turn. At first he beamed gently upon the master who soon unwrapped his cloak from about himself, released the clasp, and walked on with it hanging loosely about his shoulders. Soon the Sun shone forth in his full glory and the wandering master, before he had gone many steps, was glad to throw the cloak right off his back hence to complete his journey more lightly clad. As the North Wind discovered much to his chagrin, persuasion near always trumps force.

21. The Master and his Otiose Disciples

A master, wise and industrious, had two otiose disciples whom he kept hard at work to break them of their habitual loafing. They were not allowed to lie long abed in the mornings, but the master had them up and doing chores just as soon as the cock would crow. They disliked intensely having to awaken at such an hour, especially in wintertime, and they thought that if it were not for the cock waking up their master so horribly early they could stay longer in the warmth of their beds. So, on a certain day they chased after the bird, caught it, and wrung its neck. Assuming victory the indolent disciples were not prepared for the consequences of their deeds. For what happened was that their master, not hearing the cock's crow as usual, awakened them even earlier than ever and set them to work in the middle of the night.

Legends of the Masters

22. The Vainglorious Disciple and the Milk Pail

A master's vainglorious disciple had been out to milk the cows and was returning carrying a pail of milk upon his head in an attempt to perfect his posture. As he walked along he fell to musing after a fashion. "The milk in this pail will provide me with cream," he thought, "which I will make into butter and take to market to sell. With the money I make I shall buy a number of freshly laid eggs and these when hatched will produce chickens. By and by I shall have quite a large poultry-yard, then I shall sell some of my fowls and with the money which they will bring in I will buy myself a new bow with which I will train day and night. Once I have mastered the bow I shall take it to the faire. There I shall fire a perfect shot with the swiftest, straightest arrow and thus win a ribbon from the magistrate's comely daughter. She shall behold my handsome physique and pine after me but I shall haughtily toss my head and have nothing to say to her." Forgetting all about the pail and suiting the action to the thought, the vainglorious disciple tossed his head. Down went the pail. All the milk was spilled onto the ground, his dreams vanishing in a moment.

23. The Master, the Merchant, and the Thief

A master and a merchant became great friends. Seeking protection on the road where he went to peddle his wares, the merchant begged the master for succor and they agreed to travel together. At nightfall the merchant whose wares were quite valuable climbed up into the branches of a tree to sleep, while the master curled himself up alongside his cloak and sword inside the tree trunk which was hollow. Early in the morning the merchant awoke, stretched and yawned. Sunrise that day was so inspiring that he broke into song. A passing thief heard the commotion and, wishing to rob the merchant of his treasures, came and stood under the tree. There he asked the merchant to come down. "I should so like," said he, "to make the acquaintance of one who has such a delightful voice." The merchant upon discerning the other's intent replied, "Would you just wake my friend who sleeps at the foot of the tree? He will let you climb upon his shoulders and boost you up." The thief accordingly rapped on the trunk when suddenly out rushed the master who chopped him into pieces with his sword.

24. The Blind Master and the Cub

There was once a blind master who had so brilliant a sense of touch that when any animal was put into his hands he could tell what it was merely by the feel of it. One day a wolf's cub was given to him by his disciples who asked him what he thought it was. He felt it for some moments and then said, "Indeed, I am not sure whether this is a wolf's cub or a fox's, but this I know—it would never do to trust it in a sheepfold. Heed my words, wise disciples, evil tendencies are early shown."

25. The Master and the Thirsty Hooligan

A gang of outlaws had been terrorizing the villagers so their magistrate sought out a master to disrupt the band and drive them away. Alas, when the master arrived he quickly found himself surrounded and outmatched by the gang who trussed him up and tossed him down a well so deep that despite the fact that he was able to escape his bonds he was unable to get back out again, for they had removed the rope and bucket. By and by one of the hooligans became thirsty and approached the well. Seeing the master inside, the outlaw asked him if the water was good to drink. "Good?" replied the master, "it is by far the best water I have ever tasted in all my life, most refreshing indeed. Do not take my word for it, my friend, come on down and try it for yourself."

The hooligan, thinking of nothing but the prospect of quenching his thirst, jumped right in at once. When he had had enough to drink, the hooligan looked about like the master for some way of getting back out of the well but could find none for the walls were slick and high. Presently the master said, "I have an idea. You brace yourself firmly against the side of the well and then I shall climb up onto your back. From there, by stepping upon your shoulders I can get out. When I am out of the well, I will help you escape too." The hooligan did as he was bid and the master nimbly climbed onto his back and so out of the well… and then he serenely began walking away.

The hooligan called loudly after him and reminded the master of his promise of assistance. Instead of lending a hand the master merely turned and said, "If you had as much sense in your head as you have hair in your beard you would not have got into the well without making certain that you could get back out again."

26. The Disciple and the Cook

A master once invited a number of his friends and acquaintances to a banquet. His disciple thought that the event would be a good opportunity to invite another student, a friend of his, so he went to him and said, "My master is giving a feast. There will be a fine spread so come and dine with me tonight." The disciple thus invited came and when he saw the preparations being made in the kitchen he said to himself, "My word, I am in luck. I shall take care to eat enough this night to last me two or three days." At that moment the cook caught sight of him and, in his annoyance at seeing a strange person in the kitchen, caught him up and threw him out of the window.

After a nasty fall the disciple gathered himself and limped away as quickly as he could. Presently some other students met him along his painful journey and said, "Well, what sort of a dinner did you receive?" To which he replied, "I had a splendid time. The wine was so good, and I drank so much of it, that I really do not remember how I got out of the house!" While he may have saved face with his friends by his witty reply, the young man had indeed learned to be reticent of favors bestowed at the expense of others.

27. The Drowning Disciple and his Negligent Master

A young disciple who was bathing in a river and got out of his depth was in great danger drowning for he had not yet learned how to swim. His master who was passing along the road heard his cries for help and went to the riverside where he began to scold his charge for being so careless as to get into deep water, yet made no attempt to help pull him out. "Oh master," cried the boy, "please help me first and scold me afterwards." Thus the negligent master remembered the lesson of giving assistance not advice in a crisis and placed a charge upon himself to change his ways, one which he carried out for the rest of his days.

28. Two Masters and a Thief

Two masters tested themselves one against the other. Their skills were great, so the battle was long, fierce, and hard-fought. At length both of them were exhausted, lying upon the ground severely wounded and gasping for breath. A sly thief had all the while been prowling around, watching the fight. When he saw the combatants too weak to move, he slipped in, seized all their worldly possessions, and ran off with them. As the masters looked on helplessly, one said unto the other, "Here we have been mauling each other all this while and no one the better for it except the thief!" Never again did these two masters compete, but rather became fast friends and allies.

29. The Master and the Inept Doctor

A certain master fell sick and took to his bed. He consulted a number of doctors from time to time and they all, with one exception, told him that his life was in no immediate danger but that his illness would probably linger for a considerable time. The one who took a different view of his case, but who was also the last to be consulted, bade him prepare for the worst. "You have not but twenty-four hours to live," he said, "and I fear that I can do nothing." As it turned out, however, the inept doctor was quite wrong, for at the end of a few days the sick master quitted his bed and took a walk abroad.

In the course of his stroll, hale but pale as a specter, the master met up with the quack doctor who had prophesied his death. "Dear me," said the latter, "how do you do? You are fresh from the afterworld, no doubt, as it shows upon your complexion. Pray, how are our departed friends getting on there?" "Most comfortably," replied the master, "for they have drunk the water of oblivion and have forgotten all the troubles of life. You should know, however, that just before I left the authorities were making arrangements to prosecute all doctors upon the earth because they would not let sick men die in the course of nature, but used their healing arts to keep them alive. They were going to charge you along with the rest until I assured them that you were no doctor, merely an impostor."

30. The Two Bags

The master spoke to his disciples, "Every man carries two bags about with him, one in front and one behind, and both are packed full of faults. The satchel in front contains his neighbors' imperfections, whereas the one behind holds his own. Hence it is that men do not see their own faults, but never fail to perceive those of others around them. Wise is the man who flips the bags around and focuses foremost on perfecting himself rather than upon illuminating the failings of others."

31. The Disciple and the Filberts

A young disciple put his hand into a jar of filberts and grasped as many in his fist as he could possibly hold. When he tried to pull it out again, he found that he could not do so, for the neck of the jar was too small to allow the passage of so large a handful. Unwilling to lose the nuts but equally unable to withdraw his hand, he burst into tears. The master, who saw where the trouble lay, said to him, "Come, my boy, do not be so greedy. Be content with half the amount and you will be able to pull your hand out without difficulty. Eschew overindulgence in all things and you shall be much the happier for it."

32. Two Masters at the Spring

One hot and thirsty day in the height of summer two masters came down to a fresh, clear spring at the same moment to drink. In a trice they were quarrelling as to who should slake their thirst first. The quarrel soon became a fight and they attacked one another with the utmost fury. Presently, stopping for a moment to take breath, they spotted a convergence of vultures seated on a rock above evidently waiting for one of them to be killed whereupon they would fly down and feed on the carcass. The sight of these scavengers sobered them at once and they made up their quarrel, saying, "We had much better be friends than fight and become sustenance for the vultures."

33. A Disciple on the Housetop

Attracted by flora that grew in the thatched roof, a nimble disciple climbed up on top of an outhouse to pick wildflowers for his sweetheart. Looking around he caught sight of a master who he knew was a harsh taskmaster passing below and jeered at him knowing that since the master could not reach him he would be safe from reprisal. The master only looked up and said, "I hear you my young friend but it is not you who mock me. Rather it is the roof upon which you are standing that reflects upon you."

34. The Master and the Viper

One winter a kindhearted master found a viper stiff and numb with cold. With an overabundance of pity for the frozen serpent, the master picked it up and placed it against his bosom as diversion from the cold. The viper was no sooner revived by the man's warmth than it turned upon its benefactor and inflicted a fatal bite upon him. As the unfortunate master lay dying he cried, "I have only got what I deserved, for taking compassion on so villainous a creature." In passing he learned that kindness is squandered upon evil.

35. The Master and the Whetstone

A master sat on a log sharpening his sword with skillful strokes of his whetstone when a disciple happened by. Seeing what the master was at the disciple asked, "Why are you doing that, pray tell? We are not at war and there are no other dangers lurking at hand that I can see." "Tis true, my friend," replied the master, "but the instant that my life is in danger I shall need of my blade. Keen or dull, there will be no time to sharpen it in the heat of battle."

36. A Disciple and the Fearsome Master

A certain young disciple who had never seen a blooded warrior met one day a most fearsome master and was so terrified at the very sight of him that he was near ready to expire with fear. Terrified at the maser's approach, the disciple swiftly ran the other way. After a time he met the master again and was still rather frightened, but not nearly so much as he had been at their first encounter hence was able to stand his ground and observe the warrior as he strode by. When he saw him for the third time, the disciple was so far from being afraid that he went up to the fearsome master and began to speak with him as if he had known him all his life.

37. The Townsmen and the Brigands

There was a long-running skirmish between the inhabitants of a certain town and a vicious gang of brigands who incessantly preyed upon them. In every encounter the townsman got the worst of it, numbers of them being debased or killed with each confrontation. Lacking a master to protect them, the townsmen called a council of war in which an oldster got up and said, "Tis no wonder that we are always beaten, for we have no generals to plan our battles and direct our movements on the field." Acting upon his advice, they selected from among their numbers the biggest and strongest of the townsmen to be their leaders. These in turn, in order to be distinguished from the rank and file, provided themselves with iron helmets bearing large plumes of peacock feathers. They then led out the townsmen to battle, confident of victory. But, as fate would have it, they were defeated as usual. Soon the ferocity of the brigand's attack sent the townsfolk scampering as fast as they could to the safety of their hovels. All made their way to shelter without difficulty except for the leaders who were so hampered by the badges of their rank that they could not see nor move quickly and fell easy victims to their pursuers.

38. The Wagoner and the Master

A wagoner was driving his team along a muddy lane with a full load behind them when the wheels sank so deep into the mire that he became stuck. No efforts of his team of horses could move the wagon. As the hapless wagoner stood there looking helplessly on and calling loudly at intervals for assistance a master appeared walking along the trail. Observing the spectacle before him, the master approached and said, "Put your shoulder to the wheel, man, and goad on your horses. Only then may you call upon my aid. If you will not lift a finger to help yourself, how can you expect anyone else to come to your rescue?"

39. The Image Seller and the Master

A certain man made a wooden image and exposed it for sale in the marketplace. As he could secure no offers to buy it, however, he devised a plan to try to attract a purchaser by proclaiming the virtues of his idol. Wandering up and down the market he cried, "A god for sale! A god for sale! Who would buy a god who will bring you luck, affirm your life, and keep you lucky even unto your dotage!" Presently a master who had overheard the peddler's appeal stopped the image seller and asked, "If your god is all that you make him out to be, how is it that you do not keep him for yourself and make the most of his blessings?" "Tis an excellent question, my friend, and I shall tell you why," the image seller replied. "He brings gain, it is true, but he takes his time about it whereas I desire affluence at once." Knowing that fortune favors those with the fortitude to postpone gratification, the master immediately grasped the image seller's temperament, shook his head, and walked away.

40. The Cavalryman, his Horse, and the Master

A certain cavalryman gave his horse a plentiful supply of feed in time of war and tended to it with the utmost care, for he wished his steed to be strong enough to endure the hardships of the field, running swift and sure when need arose to engage the enemy or escape the reach of danger. But when the war was over he employed his beast for all sorts of drudgery, bestowing but little attention upon the poor animal and giving it, moreover, nothing but chaff to eat. The time came when war broke out once again and the cavalryman saddled and bridled his horse, and, having put on it his heavy coat of mail mounted him to ride off and take the field. Alas the poor half-starved beast sank down under his weight and could no longer rise. A passing master exclaimed, "You will have to go into battle on foot this time. Thanks to hard work and bad food you have turned your once noble beast from a horse into an ass and you cannot in a moment turn him back into a horse again."

41. Three Brigands and a Guileful Master

Three brigands took a room at an inn, closely watched by a master who longed to subdue them but who felt that he was no match for all three at once so long as they kept together. Since direct action would be imprudent, the guileful master settled upon another course. This he began by false whispers and malicious hints dropped in the common room so as to foment jealousies and distrust amongst his foes. This stratagem succeeded so well that ere long the brigands grew cold and unfriendly toward one another, and finally avoided each other altogether, each one going off by himself to settle in a room apart. No sooner did the master see this than he fell upon them one-by-one, killed each in turn, and carried their heads in a knapsack back to the magistrate to earn the publicized reward for dispatching them.

42. The Horse and His Rider

A certain young disciple who fancied himself something of a horseman mounted a horse which had not been properly broken in, hence was exceedingly difficult to control. No sooner did the horse feel the disciple's weight in the saddle than he bolted, leapt the stable fence, and took off down the road at a full gallop. Try as he might, nothing that the hapless disciple tried would slow his runaway steed. The rider's master met him in the road during his headlong flight and called out in surprise, "Where are you off to in such a hurry?" To which the disciple, pointing to the horse replied breathlessly, "I have no idea. Ask him!" By the time the mount came to a stop of its own accord the disciple had learned the wisdom of his master's long-stated injunction to thoughtfully consider his environment before rashly leaping into action.

43. The Elderly Master and his Churlish Liege Lord

A master who had served his liege lord long and well, and who had defended the wealthy man from many an adversary in his time, began to lose his strength and speed owing to advanced age. One day the master and his liege were set upon by brigands who coveted their treasures. While the master set about him with fury, his strength soon failed and the brigands were able to abscond with the nobleman's carriage and escape with all the valuables contained therein. Stranded by the roadside the liege began to scold him severely, but the master interrupted, "My will is as strong as ever, my lord, but my body is old and feeble. Were you compassionate and not a churl you would seek to honor me for what I have been instead of abusing me for what I am today."

44. The Compassionate Master and the Wolf

A certain compassionate master found a wolf's cub wandering through his pastures and, having pity for the stray, took it home to rear along with his dogs. When the cub grew to its full size, if ever a wolf stole a sheep from the flock it would join the dogs in hunting the perpetrator down. In the course of such events there were times when the other dogs would fail to catch the thief, however, and abandoning their pursuit would return home. This wolf would on such occasions continue the chase by itself and when it overtook the culprit stop and share a feast with him before returning to its master's abode. If some time passed without a sheep being carried off by other wolves the ungrateful young wolf would steal one itself and share its plunder with the dogs. The master's suspicions were aroused by odd disappearances and one day he caught the young wolf in the act whereupon he fastened a rope around its neck. "Fool you are," the master pronounced as he hung the young wolf on the nearest tree, "to embrace your base nature and thus betray the one who succors you."

45. The False Prophet and the Master

A prophet sat in the marketplace where he earned his keep by telling the fortunes of all who cared to engage his services. Suddenly there came running up a townsman who told the prophet that his house had been broken into by thieves and that they had made off with all of his worldly possessions. The prophet was up in a moment and rushed off, tearing his hair and calling down curses upon the heads of the miscreants. The bystanders were much amused at this display. A master among them said, "Our friend professes to know the fate of others, but it seems he is not clever enough to perceive what is in store for himself." Before the vigilant, false prophets are soon revealed.

46. The Captured Drummer

A disciple marched into battle alongside his master, banging warlike tunes upon a drum in hopes of stirring the hearts of his comrades. Alas, despite valorous effort his side was overcome and his master slain before his very eyes. Being captured by the enemy, he begged for his life, pleading, "Do not put me to death, I have killed no one. Indeed, I am no master, have no weapons, but carry only my drum that you see here with me." Undaunted, his captors replied, "That is only the more reason why we should take your life, for though you do not fight yourself you stir up others to do so." And then they struck off his head.

47. The Disciple, the Thief, and the Magistrate

A disciple engaged in horseplay inadvertently broke his master's favorite vase. Burying the shards in the woods he devised a stratagem to shift the blame to a notorious thief whom he charged with pilfering the missing urn. The thief, innocent of this particular crime, denied any wrongdoing. And so it came that the case was brought before the magistrate. When he had heard the evidence on both sides, he pronounced judgment. "I am uncertain that you ever lost the vase as you claim young disciple," declared the magistrate, "but all the same I believe that you, thief, are guilty of this crime despite of all your denials." In this the magistrate made clear the import of a man's reputation, for the dishonest gain no credit even when they act scrupulously.

48. The One-Eyed Master

After a life spent in battle a master found himself blinded in one eye from a sword blow that scored across his face. Fearful that his enemies could take advantage of this weakness and ambush him he moved to the seashore, keeping the water at his back and his one good eye turned towards the land. In this fashion he believed that he would be able to perceive any approaching danger and fight or flee as whatever be his need. As it fell out, however, a rival rowing along the shore spied him and shot an arrow at the one-eyed master, by which he was mortally wounded. As he lay dying, the master thought to himself, "Wretch that I am! I bethought me of the dangers of the land, whence none assailed me. But, I feared no peril from the sea yet thence has come my ruin." Too late the one-eyed master learned the lesson that misfortune often assails us from unexpected quarter."

49. The Starving Master and the Jewel

Lost in the woods a certain master set about him for something to eat. He tried and he tried, but nothing but sticks and stones could he find. Suddenly he turned up a jewel buried in the underbrush that had by chance been dropped there. "Ho!" said he, "a fine thing you are, no doubt, and had your owner found you great would his joy have been. But for me, alas, give me a single morsel of bread before all the jewels in the world." In wont of sustenance, wealth unspent has no meaning.

50. The Fool and the Master

One fine sunny day in the heart of winter a master was busy drying his store of grain which had got dangerously damp during a long rain spell thence become prone to rot. Presently along came a fool who knocked at his door and begged him for a few kernels of corn to eat, "For," said the simpleton, "I am all but starving." The master stopped work for a moment to reply, "What were you doing with yourself all last summer, my friend? Did you not collect a store of food for the long winter?" "The fact is," replied the fool, "I was so busy singing that I had not the time for such toil." "If you spent the summer singing," replied the master with revulsion, "you cannot do better than spend the winter dancing. Perhaps that will bring food for your table." Chuckling, he turned his back on the fool and went on with his work knowing that fate provides for those who fend for themselves.

Legends of the Masters

51. The Cobbler turned Doctor and the Master

A very unskillful cobbler, finding himself unable to make a living at his trade, gave up fabricating shoes and mending boots and took to doctoring instead. To acquire clientele, he gave out that he had stumbled upon the secret of a universal antidote against all poisons. Quite soon he had attained no small reputation amongst a certain master's disciples thanks to his talent for puffing himself up. One day, however, the cobbler himself fell very ill and the master who lived nearby thought that he would take the opportunity to test the true value of the supposed doctor's remedy. Calling, therefore for a cup, he poured out a dose of the antidote and under presence of mixing it with poison added a little wine into the mix. Then, he commanded the doctor to drink. Terrified, the cobbler confessed that he knew nothing whatsoever about medicine and that his antidote was worthless. The master then summoned his disciples and proclaimed unto them, "What folly could be greater than yours? Here is this cobbler to whom no one will send his boots for repair and yet you have not hesitated to entrust him with your very lives!"

52. The Master, the Disciple, and the Plane Tree

A master and his disciple were walking along a bare and dusty road in the heat of a summer's day. Coming presently to a plane tree, they joyfully turned aside from their trek to shelter themselves from the burning rays of the sun by resting in the deep shade of the tree's spreading branches. As they relaxed, looking up into the tree, the disciple remarked to his master, "What a useless tree the Plane is! It bears no fruit and is of no service to man at all." He began to say more but his master interjected, "We come and take shelter from the scorching sun and then in the very act of enjoying the cool shade call our benefactor worthless. Meet not a valued service with such ingratitude!"

53. The Master and the Hare

A master hunting in the woods came across a sleeping hare, grabbed a hold, and was just about to kill it for his stewpot when he caught sight of a passing stag. Dropping the hare, he at once made for the larger game. But, finding after a long chase that he could not get close enough to the stag to take a shot, the master abandoned the attempt, deciding instead to come back for the hare. When he reached the spot where it had slept, however, he discovered that the rabbit was nowhere to be seen, thus had to go home without dinner. "It serves me right," he mused aloud. "I should have been content with what I had at hand, instead of yearning after a better prize. It is prudent to take comfort in what is readily at hand rather than reach for the unobtainable and have naught."

54. The Disciple and his two Sweethearts

A disciple of middle age, whose hair was beginning to turn grey, had two sweethearts—an older woman and a younger one. The elder of the two did not like having a lover who looked so much younger than herself, so whenever he came to see her she would take advantage of their tryst to pull the dark hairs out of his head, thus to make him look old. The younger lover, on the other hand, did not like him to look so much older than herself and equally took every opportunity to pull out the grey hairs in order to make him look young. Between them they left not a hair in his head, hence the hapless disciple became perfectly bald. In the course of these events he learned, to his immense humiliation, that in an attempt to please both of his sweethearts he had satisfied no one at all, least of all himself.

55. The Master and the Bandit Lord

The leader of a ruthless gang of bandits who had just enjoyed a good meal and much fine wine was in a playful mood when he caught sight of a master lying flat against the ground spying upon him. Realizing that the master must have been lurking there for some time in hopes of collecting the bounty that lay upon his own head he thought to find sport with the other man. So, the bandit lord he stalked up to the master and proclaimed loudly enough for his men to hear, "Aha, I have found you hiding there, rapscallion, but if you can say three things to me, the truth of which cannot be disputed, my men and I will spare your life." The quick-witted master thought for a moment and then replied, "First, it is a pity that you saw me. Second, I was a fool to let myself be seen. Thirdly, truth be told, we all hate bandits because you incessantly make unprovoked attacks upon us." The bandit lord replied, "Well, what you say is true enough. You have bested me this time and may go in peace."

56. The Master and the Fearsome Warrior

A certain master went up into the hills to get some sport with his bow but instead of the game animals for which he was searching he came upon a fearsome warrior instead. The man was tall of stature, long of limb, and armored from head to foot with leather and mail. Upon spotting the approaching master, the warrior beat his sword against his shield, shouting a challenge that made clear he wished to duel. The master carried neither sword nor shield, and neither did he wear a coat of mail, yet undaunted he shot the warrior with an arrow, saying, "There, you see what my messenger can do. Just you wait a moment and I shall tackle you myself." The warrior, however, when he felt the sting of the hunting arrow through his armor ran away as fast as his legs could carry him. A fellow warrior who had witnessed the entire encounter, shouted after the running man, "Come, do not be a coward. Why do you not stay and show fight?" But as the fearsome warrior ran past he replied, "You will not convince me to stay, not you. Why when he sends a messenger like that before him, he must himself be a terrible fellow to battle."

57. The Stargazing Disciple

There was a certain disciple whose habit it was to go out at night and observe the stars. One evening, as he was walking outside the town gates in the gathering darkness he gazed up absorbed into the sky rather than looking where he was going. In the course of his travel he tripped and fell into a dry well, landing in a heap at the bottom. As he lay there groaning his master happened by and heard his cries for help. Coming to the edge of the well the master looked down and, on learning what had happened, said, "If you really mean to say that you were looking so hard at the sky that you did not even see where your feet were carrying you along the ground, it appears to me that you deserve all you have received. Heed the lesson and get yourself up out of the well."

58. By the Company he Keeps

A master who wanted to buy horse went to market and, coming across a likely-looking steed, arranged with the owner that he should be allowed to take him home on a trial basis to see what the beast was like. When he reached his residence the master put the horse into his stable along with the rest of his herd. The newcomer took a look round and immediately took its place next to the laziest and greediest beast in the entire stable. When the master saw this he immediately put a halter on the newcomer, led him off, and handed him back over to his owner again. The latter was a good deal surprised to see his horse back so soon, asking, "Do you mean to say you have tested him already and found him wanting?" "I have no wish to put him through any more tests," replied the master. "I could readily enough discern what sort of beast he is from the companion he chose for himself."

59. The Bald Master

A master who had lost all his hair took to wearing a wig to preserve his vanity. One rainy day he went out to practice in the courtyard with his disciples. It was blowing rather hard at the time and events had not progressed far before a gust of wind caught up his hat and carried it off along with the wig, much to the amusement of his disciples who had not known he was bald. Unabashed, the master entered into the joke saying, "Ah, well! The hair that wig is made of did not stick to the head upon which it grew. 'Tis truly no wonder it will not stick to mine."

60. The Master and his Dog

A master's dog was playing in the yard when it misjudged a leap and fell into a deep well. Failing to retrieve his pet by means of a rope and a bucket, the master lowered himself down into the well in order to fetch it up directly. But, the dog panicked. Thinking that the man had come to make sure of drowning it, the dog bit its master as soon as he came within reach, hurting him a good deal in so doing. With that result that the master left his dog to its fate. Climbing back out of the well he remarked, "It serves me quite right for trying to save so determined a suicide."

61. A Warrior in Love

A mighty, but ill-tempered warrior fell deeply in love with a certain master's daughter and wanted with all his heart to marry her, but her father was unwilling to give her to so fearsome a husband. However much he loathed him, the master was deathly afraid to insult the armed and armored warrior so he said, "I believe that you will make a very good husband for my daughter, but I cannot consent to your union unless you allow me to break your spear in twain and beat your sword into a plow shear, for my daughter is terribly afraid of these weapons." The warrior was so much in love that he readily agreed that all that had been proposed should be done. After the warrior had been disarmed, however, the master had no more reason for fear and drove him away with his staff.

62. Brigands, the Townsfolk, and the Master

A company of brigands sent a deputation to the village with proposals for a lasting peace between them, on condition of their giving up their warriors to immediate death. The foolish townsfolk were about to agree to these outrageous terms when a master, whose years had brought him wisdom, interfered and said, "How can we expect to live at peace with you? Why, even with the warriors at hand to protect us we are never secure from your murderous attacks!" Buoyed by the master's wisdom, the townsfolk rejected the brigand's terms and sent them packing.

Legends of the Masters

63. The Disciple and the Swan

The swan is said to sing but once in its life—when it knows that it is about to die. A certain disciple, who had heard of the song of the swan, one day saw one of these birds for sale in the marketplace, bought it, and took it home with him. A few nights later he had some friends to dinner, produced the swan, and bade it sing for their entertainment. Alas, the swan remained silent. In course of time when it had grown old and weak the bird became aware of its approaching demise, thence broke into a sweet, sad song. When its owner heard it, he said angrily, "If the creature only sings when it is about to die, what a fool I was that day I wanted to hear its song! I ought to have sought to ring its neck instead of merely inviting it to sing."

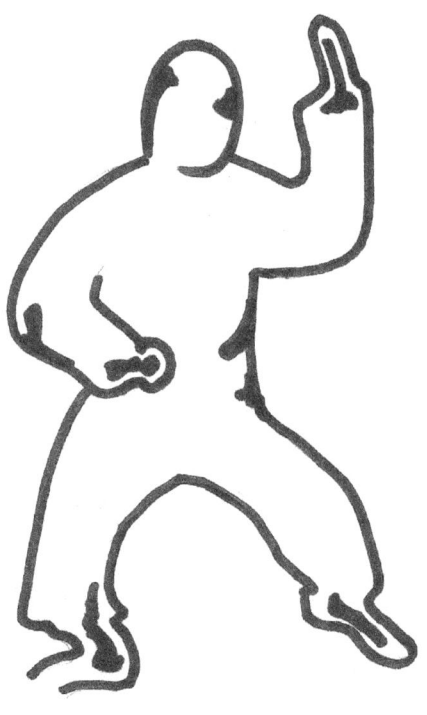

64. The Master, the Disciple, and the Ant

A certain disciple once saw a ship in the harbor catch flame and go down with all its crew. He then railed against the injustice of the gods, saying "They care nothing for a man's character, but let the good and the bad perish together as one." As chance would have it there was an anthill close by where he stood and just as he spoke he was bitten upon the toe by an ant. Turning in a temper to the anthill he stamped upon it and crushed hundreds of unoffending insects along with the perpetrator. His master who had been standing nearby and overseen everything belabored the disciple with his staff, saying as he did so, "You dissembler, charlatan, where is your sense of justice now? While some men's deeds lack merit, the hypocrite abases himself as the lowest of the low."

65. The Imposter

A certain disciple fell ill and, being in a very bad way, he made a vow that he would sacrifice a hundred oxen to the gods if they would but grant him a return to health. Wishing to see how he would keep his vow, they caused him to recover in a short time. Now, he had not an ox in the world, and even his master's stables were not so full, so he made a hundred little oxen out of tallow and offered them up on an altar at the same time saying, "Ye gods, I call upon you to witness that I have discharged my vow." The embittered gods determined to be even with him, so they sent this disciple a dream in which he was bidden to travel to a distant town there to fetch a hundred coins of purest silver which he would find there. Hastening in great excitement toward the village he fell in with a band of robbers along the road who seized him, trussed him up, and carried him off to sell as a slave. At the slave auction, as fate would have it, a hundred silver coins was the sum he fetched. The disciple laid low learned that woe is he who utters false promises.

66. The Bandit Chief and his Disciples

Three bandits went out seeking their fortunes together. Thanks to the deviousness of their leader they had soon taken a large booty which the chief requested one of his disciples to divide amongst them. This disciple divided the loot into three equal parts and modestly begged the others to take their choice of piles at which point the bandit chief, bursting with fury, sprang upon the disciple and stabbed him through the heart with his knife. Then, glaring at the remaining disciple he bade him make a fresh division. The second disciple gathered almost the whole of the bounty in one great heap for the leader's share, leaving only a few coins residual for himself. "My dear friend," said the bandit chief, "how did you get the knack of banditry so well?" The disciple replied, "Oh, I took a lesson from my brother." This disciple had discerned the lesson that happy is he who learns from the misfortunes of others.

67. The Old Master and The Grim Reaper

An old master cut himself a bundle of sticks with which to set fire and warm his hearth and started to carry them home. He had a long way to go and no beast of burden to share his load hence was tired out before he had traveled much more than halfway. Casting his bundle on the ground, he sullenly called upon death to come and release him from his life of endless toil. The words were scarcely out of his mouth when, much to the old master's dismay, The Grim Reaper himself appeared before him and professed his readiness to serve. Encountering the skeletal visage the old master was nearly frightened beyond his wits, but he had enough presence of mind to stammer out, "Good sir, if you would be so kind, pray help me up with my burden again." In his dotage the old master learned the lesson that the wise men are prudent of what they wish for.

68. The Disciple and his Shadow

A disciple who was roaming about his master's courtyard as the sun was getting low in the sky was much impressed by the size of his shadow. He said to himself, "I had no idea I was so big. Fancy my being afraid of the master. Why, I, not he, deserve to be the leader of our clan." With headstrong certitude he strutted about the place berating those around him as if there could be no doubt at all of his superiority. Just then the master, irked by his disciple's antics, struck him a mighty blow that knocked him off his feet. "Alas," the stunned disciple cried, "had I not lost sight of the truth, I should not have been brought low by my fancies."

69. The Miser and the Master

A miser sold everything he owned in the world for coin. He then proceeded to melt his hoard down into a single lump of gold which he secretly buried in a field under the cover of night. Every day thereafter he made a pilgrimage to this field to gaze upon his treasure and would often spend long hours there gloating over his prize. One of the miser's servants noticed these frequent visits and, one day, followed after him discovering the miser's secret. Awaiting his opportunity, the servant snuck out in the dead of night, dug up the gold, and stole it for himself. When on the next day the miser visited the place as usual, he discovered naught but an empty hole. Treasure gone, he fell to tearing his hair and wailing after his loss. In this condition he was discovered by one of his neighbors, a master, who was concerned for his health asked him what his trouble was. The miser told the master of his misfortune, to which his neighbor replied, "Do not take it so much to heart, my friend. Put a brick into the hole, fill it back up with dirt, and look upon it every day as has been your wont. You will not be any worse off than before, for even when you had your lump of gold it was of no earthly use to you."

70. Disciples at the River

A number of disciples assembled on the bank of a river and wanted to drink but the current was so strong and the water looked so deep and dangerous that they did dared not do so. Instead they stood near the river's edge encouraging one another to not be afraid. At last one of them, to shame his companions and show his courage, said, "I am not one bit frightened! See, I shall step right into the water." He had no sooner acted as he had spoken when the current swept him off his feet carried him away downstream. The others cried, "Do not go and leave us! Come back and show us where we too can drink with safety." But no matter how hard he struggled against the current he made no headway so he replied, "I am afraid I cannot… yet. I have always wanted to gaze upon the sea. It seems that this current will take me there nicely. Never fear, when I come back I shall show you with pleasure."

71. The Master who lost his Spade

A master was engaged in digging a well upon his property. One day upon arriving to continue his toil he discovered his spade was no longer where he had left it the previous day. Believing that it may have been stolen by one of his disciples, the master questioned them closely yet they one and all denied any knowledge of the crime. The master was not convinced of the sincerity of their denials, however, hence insisted that they should all go to the town and take oath in a temple there that they were not guilty of the theft. This was because he had no great opinion of the simple country deities, but imagined rather that the thief would not pass undetected past the shrewder gods of the town. When they got inside the town's gates the first thing they heard was a crier proclaiming a reward for information about a thief who had stolen something of value from the city temple. "Well," said the master to himself, "it strikes me that I had better go back home again. If these town gods cannot detect the thieves who steal from their own temples, it is scarcely likely they can tell me who purloined my spade."

72. The Huntsman, the Master, and the Tracks of the Lion

A hunter was searching in the forest for the tracks of a lion and catching sight presently of a master engaged in felling a tree, he went up to him and asked if he had noticed a lion's footprints anywhere about or if he knew where the beast's den was hidden. The master having no small familiarity with the area answered, "If you will come with me, I will show you the lion himself." The hunter turned pale with fear as he replied, "Oh, I am not looking for the lion, but only for his tracks."

73. The Serpent, the Eagle, and the Master

An eagle swooped down upon a serpent and seized it up in his talons with the intention of carrying it off and devouring it. Alas, the serpent was too quick for the mighty bird and had its coils round him in a moment and then there ensued a life-and-death struggle between the two. A certain master was traveling along a country road when he bore witness to the encounter and, having a certain disdain for snakes, came to the assistance of the eagle. After a struggle he succeeded in freeing the bird from the serpent's grasp, thus enabling the eagle's escape. Unbeknownst to the master the serpent spat some of his poison into his drinking-horn to avenge his mistreatment by the man. Heated with his exertions, the master was about to slake his thirst with a draught from the horn when the eagle knocked it from his hand, spilling its contents upon the ground, for even the avian instinctively know that one good turn deserves another.

74. The Disciple Chasing a Brigand

A certain master's disciple was chasing a brigand whom he had caught pilfering. As he ran the disciple thought of what a fine fellow he was, what strong legs he had, and how quickly they covered the ground. "Now, there is this brigand," he said to himself, "what a poor creature he is, for he is no match for me and knowing so he near soils himself as he runs away." But the brigand looked round just then and said, "Do not you imagine I am running away from you, my friend, it is your master I am afraid of." Sure enough, the disciple glanced behind and spied that his master had joined the chase.

75. The Widow and the Mendacious Disciple

A widow used to go every day to her husband's grave, there to lament her loss. A disciple who was engaged in plowing his master's land not far from the spot set eyes upon the woman's lovely visage and desired at once to have her for his wife. So, he left his plow behind and came to sit by her side. Soon he began to shed tears himself. When the widow asked him why he wept the disciple replied, "I have lately lost my wife, who was very dear to me, and these tears ease my grief." "And I," said she, "have lost my husband." And so for a while they mourned together in companionable silence. Then he said, "Since we find ourselves in the same condition, you and I, shall we not do well to marry and live together? I shall take the place of your dead husband while you that of my departed wife."

After some small consideration the widow consented to the plan, which indeed seemed reasonable enough, and they dried their tears. Meanwhile, a thief had come along and stolen the oxen which the disciple had abandoned along with his plow. Upon discovering the theft, the disciple rent his clothing and loudly bewailed his loss. When the widow heard his cries she came running and asked, "You are weeping still?" to which the disciple without thought replied, "Yes, and I mean it this time." His hoax discovered, the comely widow slapped the disciple stoutly about the cheek and headed directly to her home, never to speak to the mendacious young man again.

76. The Master and the Horseman

A master went out into the woods after game and soon succeeded in catching a fat hare which he was carrying home with him when he met a man on horseback. The horseman said, "I see you have had some sport, sir," and offered to buy it. The master readily agreed, for the price was fair and he already had enough to eat, but the horseman had no sooner got the hare in his hands then he set spurs to his horse and headed off at full gallop. The master rushed after the devious horseman for some little distance but soon gave up trying to overtake the rider as he knew that it could not be done. To save his face, however, the master called after him as loud as he could, "All right sir, all right. Take your hare; it was meant as a present for you all along."

 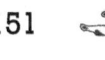

77. The Master who was an Oracle

A certain master was said to be blessed with the ability to divine the future. A rogue, upon hearing this rumor, laid a wager that he would prove the oracle untrustworthy by receiving from him a false reply to an inquiry. So, he scheduled a rendezvous and went to the master's abode on the appointed day with a small bird in his hand, which he concealed under the folds of his cloak. There he asked whether what he held in his hand were alive or dead. If the master said "dead," he meant to produce the bird alive, whereas if the reply was "alive," he intended to crush the creature thus to show it to be dead. But the master was far too clever for him, for the answer the rogue received was, "Stranger, whether the thing that you hold in your hand be alive or dead is a matter that depends entirely upon your own will." Thus the master proved that he was indeed a prophet.

78. The Wily Master

A master entering an inn came across a notorious bandit seated at the table, but he did not dare to attack the outlaw for the master carried no weapon, not even a staff, and feared that he could not prevail against the brigand's sword. His sense of justice enflamed, he felt compelled to do something and could not let the moment pass. As the direct use of force promised little success he determined to resort to artifice. Feigning friendly intent the master went up to the bandit and said unto him, "I cannot help saying how much I admire your magnificent attire. What fine threads do you wear! But, my dear friend, what in the world would compel you to carry that ugly weapon by your side? You must find it as awkward as it is unsightly. Believe me; you would do much better without it." The bandit was foolish enough to be persuaded by this flattery and tossed his weapon aside. Having now lost his only means of defense, he fell easy prey to the master who soundly beat him, trussed him up, and brought him before the magistrate for execution. The vain are easily seduced through flattery.

79. A Master, his Disciple, and the Robbers

Two men, master and disciple, were travelling on the road together when they were set upon by robbers. The disciple immediately ran away yet the master stood his ground, laying about him so lustily with his sword that even though he struck no mortal wound the robbers were fain to fly and leave the master in peace. When the peril had abated the timid disciple rushed back and, flourishing his weapon, proclaimed in a threatening voice, "Where are they? Let me get at them and I shall soon let them know the mettle of whom they have encountered." But the master shook his head forlornly and replied, "You are quite tardy, my disciple. I wish but that you had but stood by my side under duress, even if you had done no more than speak as you do now for I should have been encouraged believing truth in your words. As it is, calm yourself and put up your sword. You have no further use for it. You may delude others into thinking that you are as brave as any eminent master, but you and I both know that at the first sign of danger you will always run away a coward."

80. The Master's Indomitable Spirit

Two masters engaged in a contest before their assembled disciples, the results of which would determine once and for all who was the greater warrior. The struggle was long and fierce, each man determined to make the other submit while fortifying his own spirit in hopes to persevere. At long last the first master managed to secure the second in a stranglehold. Knowing that time was short, for he would quickly lose the contest, the second master struck his adversary a mighty blow, dislocating his ankle, then pitched his body askew with all the force of his considerable frame in an effort to wrest his neck clear of the other's grasp. As his ankle slipped its socket, the first master found that he could no longer bear the pain and with a heavy heart signaled submission. Releasing his stranglehold only to find a lifeless body atop him, the first master discovered that the second had broken his own neck attempting to escape. Having submitted to a dead man the first master hung his head in shame, for he had discovered that through indomitable spirit any victory is possible. Even for a dead man.

ABOUT THE AUTHORS

Lawrence A. Kane

Lawrence is the best-selling author of a dozen books, including an *eLit Book Awards* Bronze prize, a *Next Generation Indie Book Awards* finalist, two *USA Book News* Best Books Award finalists, and two *ForeWord Magazine* Book of the Year Award finalists. A founding technical consultant to University of New Mexico's Institute of Traditional Martial Arts, he also has written numerous articles on martial arts, self-defense, countervailing force, and related topics. He was once interviewed in English by a reporter from a Swiss newspaper for an article that was published in French, and found that oddly amusing.

Since 1970, he has studied and taught traditional Asian martial arts, medieval European combat, and modern close-quarter weapon techniques. Working stadium security part-time for 26 years he was involved in hundreds of violent altercations, but got paid to watch football. To pay the bills he develops IT strategies for an aerospace company where he gets to play with billions of dollars of other people's money and make really important decisions.

Lawrence lives in Seattle, Washington with his son Joey and wife Julie. You can contact him directly at:

lakane@ix.netcom.com

Kris Wilder

Kris Wilder is the head instructor and owner of West Seattle Karate Academy. He started practicing the martial arts at the age of fifteen. Over the years he has earned black belt rankings in three styles, *Goju-Ryu* karate (5th *dan*), tae kwon do (2nd *dan*), and judo (1st *dan*), in which he has competed in senior nationals and international tournaments. He is the author of ten books including two *USA Book News* Best Books Award finalists and a *ForeWord Magazine* Book of the Year Award finalist. He also stars in two instructional DVDs.

Kris has been blessed with the opportunity to train under skilled instructors, including Olympic athletes, state champions, national champions, and gifted martial artists who take their lineage directly from the founders of their systems. He teaches seminars worldwide, focusing on growing a person's martial technique and their understanding, whatever their art may be. Kris also serves as a National Representative for the University of New Mexico's Institute of Traditional Martial Arts.

Kris spent about 15 years in the political and public affairs area, working for campaigns from the local to national level. During this consulting career he was periodically on staff for elected officials. His work also involved lobbying and corporate affairs. He is currently a member of The Order of St. Francis (OSF); the OSF is one of many active Apostolic Christian Orders.

Kris lives in Seattle, Washington with his son Jackson. You can contact him directly at thedojo@quidnunc.net.

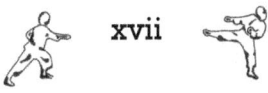

OTHER WORKS BY THE AUTHORS

Non-Fiction Books

1. <u>Sensei Mentor Teacher Coach</u> (Wilder/Kane)

   "Finally a book that will actually move the needle in closing the leadership skills gap found in all aspects of our society." – Dan Roberts, CEO and President, Ouellette & Associates

   Many books weave platitudes, promising the keys to success in leadership, secrets that will transform you into the great leader, the one. The fact of the matter is, however, that true leadership really isn't about you. It's about giving back, offering your best to others so that they can find the best in themselves. The methodologies in this book help you become the leader you were meant to be by bringing your goals and other peoples' needs together to create a powerful, combined vision. Learn how to access the deeper aspects of who you are, your unique qualities, and push them forward in actionable ways. Acquire this vital information and advance your leadership journey today

2. Dirty Ground (Kane/Wilder)

   "Fills a void in martial arts training." – Loren W. Christensen, Martial Arts Masters Hall of Fame member

   This book addresses a significant gap in most martial arts training, the tricky space that lies between sport and combat applications where you need to control a person without injuring him (or her). Techniques in this region are called "drunkle," named after the drunken uncle disrupting a family gathering. Understanding how to deal with combat, sport, and drunkle situations is vital because appropriate use of force is codified in law and actions that do not accommodate these regulations can have severe repercussions. Martial arts techniques must be adapted to best fit the situation you find yourself in. This book shows you how.

3. How to Win a Fight (Kane/Wilder)

   "It is the ultimate course in self-defense and will help you survive and get through just about any violent situation or attack." – Jeff Rivera, bestselling author

   More than three million Americans are involved in a violent physical encounter every year. Develop the fortitude to walk away when you can and prevail when you must. Defense begins by scanning your environment, recognizing hazards and escape routes, and using verbal de-escalation to defuse tense situations. If a fight is unavoidable, the authors offer clear guidance for being the victor, along with advice on legal implications, including how to handle a police interview after the altercation.

4. Lessons from the Dojo Floor (Wilder)

   "Helps each reader, from white belt to black belt, look at and understand why he or she trains." – Michael E. Odell, Isshin-Ryu Northwest Okinawa Karate Association

   In the vein of Dave Lowry, a thought provoking collection of short vignettes that entertains while it educates. Packed with straightforward, easy, and quick to read sections that range from profound to insightful to just plain amusing, anyone with an affinity for martial arts can benefit from this material.

5. Martial Arts Instruction (Kane)

   "Boeing trains hundreds of security officers, Kane's ideas will help us be more effective." – Gregory A. Gwash, Chief Security Officer, Boeing

   While the old adage, "those who can't do, teach," is not entirely true, all too often "those who can do" cannot teach effectively. This book is unique in that it offers a holistic approach to teaching martial arts; incorporating elements of educational theory and communication techniques typically overlooked in *budo* (warrior arts). Teachers will improve their abilities to motivate, educate, and retain students, while students interested in the martial arts will develop a better understanding of what instructional method best suits their needs.

6. Scaling Force (Kane/Miller)

   "If you're serious about learning how the application of physical force works—before, during and after the

fact—I cannot recommend this book highly enough." – Lieutenant Jon Lupo, New York State Police

Conflict and violence cover a broad range of behaviors, from intimidation to murder, and require an equally broad range of responses. A kind word will not resolve all situations, nor will wristlocks, punches, or even a gun. This book introduces the full range of options, from skillfully doing nothing to employing deadly force. You will understand the limits of each type of force, when specific levels may be appropriate, the circumstances under which you may have to apply them, and the potential costs, legally and personally, of your decision.

7. <u>Surviving Armed Assaults</u> (Kane)

"This book will be an invaluable resource for anyone walking the warrior's path, and anyone who is interested in this vital topic." – Lt. Col. Dave Grossman, Director, Warrior Science Group

A sad fact is that weapon-wielding thugs victimize 1,773,000 citizens every year in the United States alone. Even martial artists are not immune from this deadly threat. Consequently, self-defense training that does not consider the very real possibility of an armed attack is dangerously incomplete. Whether you live in the city or countryside, you should be both mentally and physically prepared to deal with an unprovoked armed assault at any time. Preparation must be comprehensive enough to account for the plethora of pointy objects, blunt instruments, explosive devices, and deadly projectiles that someday could be used against you. This extensive book teaches proven survival skills that can keep you safe.

8. <u>The 87 Fold Path to Being the Best Martial Artist</u> (Kane/Wilder)

   "Beware! The 87-Fold Path contains unexpected, concise blows to the head and heart... you don't have a chance, but to examine and retool your way of life." – George Rohrer, Executive and Purpose Coach, MBA, CPCC, PCC

   Despite the fact that raw materials in feudal Japan were mediocre at best, bladesmiths used innovative folding and tempering techniques to forge some of the finest swords imaginable for their samurai overlords. The process of heating and folding the metal removed impurities, while shaping and strengthening the blades to perfection. The end result was strong yet supple, beautiful and deadly. As martial artists we utilize a similar process, forging our bodies through hard work, perseverance, and repetition. The challenge is that training solely toward physical perfection is not enough. In fact, the more a practitioner knows about physical conflict, the less likely he or she is to engage in violence. Knowing how to fight is important, clearly, yet if you do not find something larger than base violence attached your efforts it becomes unsustainable, your martial arts adventure will eventually come to an end. The 87-Fold Path provides ideas for taking training beyond the physical that are uniquely tailored for the elite martial artist. This makes the martial journey more enjoyable, meaningful, and longer lasting.

9. <u>The Little Black Book of Violence</u> (Kane/Wilder)

   "This book will save lives!" – Alain Burrese, JD, former US Army 2nd Infantry Division Scout Sniper School instructor

Men commit 80 % of all violent crimes and are twice as likely to become the victims of aggressive behavior. This book is primarily written for men ages 15 to 35, and contains more than mere self-defense techniques. You will learn crucial information about street survival that most martial arts instructors don't even know. Discover how to use awareness, avoidance, and de-escalation to help stave off violence, know when it's prudent to fight, and understand how to do so effectively.

10. The Way of Kata (Kane/Wilder)

"This superb book is essential reading for all those who wish to understand the highly effective techniques, concepts, and strategies that the kata were created to record." – Iain Abernethy, British Combat Association Hall of Fame member

The ancient masters developed *kata*, or "formal exercises," as fault-tolerant methods to preserve their unique, combat-proven fighting systems. Unfortunately, they also deployed a two-track system of instruction where an outer circle of students unknowingly received modified forms with critical details or important principles omitted. Only the select inner circle that had gained a master's trust and respect would be taught *okuden waza*, the powerful hidden applications of *kata*. The theory of deciphering *kata* applications (*kaisai no genri*) was once a great mystery revealed only to trusted disciples of the ancient masters in order to protect the secrets of their systems. Even today, while the basic movements of *kata* are widely known, advanced practical applications and sophisticated techniques frequently remain hidden from the casual observer. The principles and rules for understanding *kata* are largely unknown. This groundbreaking book unveils these methods, not only teaching you how to analyze your *kata* to understand what it is trying to tell you, but also helping you to utilize your fighting techniques more effectively.

11. The Way of Martial Arts for Kids (Wilder)

"Written in a personable, engaging style that will appeal to kids and adults alike." – Laura Weller, Guitarist, *The Green Pajamas*

Based on centuries of traditions, martial arts training can be a positive experience for kids. The book helps you and yours get the most out of class. It shows how just about any child can become one of those few exemplary learners who excel in the training hall as well as in life. Written to children, it is also for parents too. After all, while the martial arts instructor knows his art, no one knows his/her child better than the parent. Together you can help your child achieve just about anything... The advice provided is straightforward, easy to understand, and written with a child-reader in mind so that it can either be studied by the child and/or read together with the parent.

12. The Way of Sanchin Kata (Wilder)

"This book has been sorely needed for generations!" – Philip Starr, National Chairman, Yiliquan Martial Arts Association

When Karate or *Ti* was first developed in Okinawa it was about using technique and extraordinary power to end a fight instantly. These old ways of generating remarkable power are still accessible, but they are

purposefully hidden in *Sanchin kata* for the truly dedicated to find. This book takes the practitioner to new depths of practice by breaking down the form piece-by-piece, body part by body part, so that the very foundation of the *kata* is revealed. Every chapter, concept, and application is accompanied by a "Test It" section, designed for you to explore and verify the *kata* for yourself. *Sanchin kata* really comes alive when you feel the thrill of having those hidden teachings speak to you across the ages through your body. Simply put, once you read this book and test what you have learned, your karate will never be the same.

13. Journey: The Martial Artist's Notebook (Kane/Wilder)

"Students who take notes progress faster and enjoy a deeper understanding than those who don't. Period."
– Loren W. Christensen, martial arts Masters Hall of Fame inductee

As martial arts students progress through the lower ranks it is extraordinarily useful for them to keep a record of what they have learned. The mere process of writing things down facilitates deeper understanding. This concept is so successful, in fact, that many schools require advanced students to complete a thesis or research project concurrent with testing for black belt (or equivalent) rank, advancing the knowledge base of the organization while simultaneously clarifying and adding depth to each practitioner's understanding of his or her art. Just as Bruce Lee's notes and essays became *Tao of Jeet Kune Do*, perhaps someday your training journal will be published for the masses, but first and foremost this notebook is by you, for you. It contains both structured and unstructured blank pages for you to take notes and make sketches that enhance your training experience. As an added bonus, there are 125 thought-provoking martial arts quotes too. This is where the deeper journey on your martial path begins...

14. The Way to Black Belt (Kane/Wilder)

"It is so good I wish I had written it myself." — *Hanshi* Patrick McCarthy, Director, International Ryukyu Karate Research Society

Cut to the very core of what it means to be successful in the martial arts. Earning a black belt can be the most rewarding experience of a lifetime, but getting there takes considerable planning. Whether your interests are in the classical styles of Asia or in today's Mixed Martial Arts, this book prepares you to meet every challenge. Whatever your age, whatever your gender, you will benefit from the wisdom of master martial artists around the globe, including Iain Abernethy, Dan Anderson, Loren Christensen, Jeff Cooper, Wim Demeere, Aaron Fields, Rory Miller, Martina Sprague, Phillip Starr, and many more, who share more than 300 years of combined training experience. Benefit from their guidance during your development into a first-class black belt.

Fiction Books

1. <u>Blinded by the Night</u> (Kane)

   "Kane's expertise in matters of mayhem shines throughout." – Steve Perry, bestselling author

   Richard Hayes is a Seattle cop. After 25 years with the PD he thinks he knows everything there is to know about predators. The dregs of society like rapists, murderers, gang bangers, and child molesters are just another day at the office. Commonplace criminals become the least of his problems when he goes hunting for a serial killer and runs into a real monster. The creature not only attacks him, but merely gets pissed off when he shoots it. In the head. Twice! Surviving that fight is only the beginning. Richard discovers that the vampire he destroyed was the ruler of an eldritch realm he never dreamed existed. By some archaic rule, having defeated the monster's sovereign in battle, Richard becomes their new king. Now he is responsible for a host of horrors who stalk the night, howl at the moon, and shamble through the darkness. But, why would these creatures willingly obey a human? When it comes to human predators, Richard is a seasoned veteran, yet with paranormal ones he is but a rookie. He must navigate a web of intrigue and survive long enough to discover how a regular guy can tangle with supernatural creatures and prevail. One mistake and things surely won't end well...

DVDs

1. <u>121 Killer Appz</u> (Wilder/Kane)

    "Quick and brutal, the way karate is meant to be." – Eric Parsons, Founder, Karate for Life Foundation

    You know the *kata*, now it is time for the applications. *Gekisai (Dai Ni)*, *Saifa*, *Seiyunchin*, *Seipai*, *Kururunfa*, *Suparinpei*, *Sanseiru*, *Shisochin*, and *Seisan kata* are covered. If you ever wondered what purpose a move from a *Goju Ryu* karate form was for, wonder no longer. This DVD contains no discussion, just a no-nonsense approach to one application after another. It is sure to provide deeper understanding to your *kata* practice and stimulate thought on determining your own applications to the *Goju Ryu* karate forms.

2. <u>Sanchin Kata: Three Battles Karate Kata</u> (Wilder)

    "A cornucopia of martial arts knowledge." – Shawn Kovacich, endurance high-kicking world record holder (as certified by the Guinness Book of World Records)

    A traditional training method for building karate power *Sanchin kata*, or Three Battles Sequence, is an ancient form that can be traced back to the roots of karate. Some consider it the missing link between Chinese kung fu and Okinawan karate. *Sanchin kata* is known to develop extraordinary quickness and generate

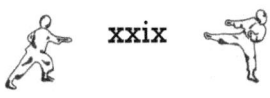

remarkable power. This program breaks down the form piece by piece, body part by body part, so that the hidden details of the *kata* are revealed. Regular practice of *Sanchin kata* conditions the body, trains correct alignment, and teaches the essential structure needed for generating power within all of your karate movements. Many karate practitioners believe that *Sanchin kata* holds the key to mastering the traditional martial arts. Though it can be one of the simplest forms to learn, it is simultaneously one of the most difficult to perfect. This DVD complements the book The Way of Sanchin Kata, providing in-depth exploration of the form, with detailed instruction of the essential posture, linking the spine, generating power, and demonstration of the complete *kata*.

3. Scaling Force (Miller/Kane)

    "Kane and Miller have been there, done that and have the t-shirt. And they're giving you their lessons learned without requiring you to pay the fee in blood they had to in order to learn them. And that is priceless." – M. Guthrie, Federal Air Marshal

    Conflict and violence cover a broad range of behaviors, from intimidation to murder, and they require an equally broad range of responses. A kind word will not resolve all situations, nor will wristlocks, punches, or even a gun. Rory Miller and Lawrence A. Kane explain and demonstrate the full range of options, from skillfully doing nothing to applying deadly force. You will learn to understand the limits of each type of force, when specific levels may be appropriate, the circumstances under which you may have to apply them, and the potential cost of your decision, legally and personally. It is vital to enter this scale at the right level, and to articulate why what you did was appropriate. If you do not know how to succeed at all six levels, there are situations in which you will have no appropriate options. More often than not, that will end badly.

www.ingramcontent.com/pod-product-compliance
Lightning Source LLC
Chambersburg PA
CBHW071500040426
42444CB00008B/1419